Stragglers

POEMS

AF451354

Trent Busch

Straggling: to stray from the road, to wander about in a scattered fashion, to be spread at irregular intervals

Cyberwit.net
HIG 45 Kaushambi Kunj, Kalindipuram
Allahabad - 211011 (U.P.) India
http://www.cyberwit.net
Tel: +(91) 9415091004
E-mail: info@cyberwit.net

To Carol

Author's Note

M.H. Abrams, General Editor of *The Norton Anthology of English Literature* remarked in his introduction to Percy Shelley that Shelley was "a poet who almost entirely lacked an audience." Would it be inaccurate to say that almost all poets in America, virtually in the world, are almost entirely without an audience? They have, we must confess, their small followings: other poet friends (who are, for the most part, without an audience themselves), their open mic evenings, their followers on Twitter, their Instagram and Facebook companions, their little books of poems.

Of course, poets aren't alone; singers, musicians, painters, photographers, actors, sculptors (not to mention ordinary men and women who have few artistic aspirations), share the same fortune. They too are stragglers who wake upon the midnight thrown back on the dead-center of themselves where no muse will every press their hearts within her hands. In W. B. Yeats' words these are the ones "whose work has come to nothing." What, then, keeps them going as they get seasons along below a Montana sky or eat plantains in a Miami furnished room, all the while trying to amaze the world with images and new ways of putting words together to make pictures or thoughts that are both alive and seeable, yet being rewarded so minimally for their trying?

Those stragglers are the subject of these poems. Perhaps we can only comfort them with Yeats' good advice to keep laboring on since they are the ones who must "exult / Because of all things known / That is most difficult."

Acknowledgements

Thanks to the editors of the following publications where poems, sometimes with different titles and in different form, first appeared:

Argestes Literary Review, "Sandwich"
Ariel, "A New Play"
artisan, "Chosen to Notice Color"
The Alembic, "Of Which We Know"
Asphodel, "The Minor Ones"
The Baltimore Review, "Lit"
Barrow Street, "Come to Nothing"
Beloit Poetry Journal, "The Great Plateau"
Bluestem, "A Handbook for Actors"
Buckle &, "Whether in a Cold Room"
Calapooya, "Exteriors"
The Chaffin Journal, "At the Cigarette Stand"
The Chariton Review, "Turner Cassity in Atlanta? I Thought He
  Was in Chicago"
The Chattahoochee Review, "Fifteen"
Chiron Review, "Janet"
Cider Press Review, "Personal"
Cimarron Review, "The Writer's Notes"
CircleShow, "Opportunity"
Common Ground Review, "In the Other Room"
Connecticut River Review, "The Funny Looking Man"
Crazyhorse, "Shelter"
Descant, "Put a Title Here"
Freshwater, "The Cold Ones"
The Gamut, "The Detectives"
Georgia Journal, "The Eyes Song"
Harpur Palate, "The Wing"

Hubbub, "Cynthia"

The Hudson Review, "Car"

Illya's Honey, "The Blank Page"

The Kerf, "Why I'm Not an Actor"

Licking River Review, "Tuesday"

The Lullwater Review, "Dorothy's Room"

Mad Poet's Review, "House Payments"

Mid-American Poetry Review, "Old Man through His Children's Eyes Remembers Papa"

Nebo, "Fall Semester"

Off the Coast, "Trial at Amherst"

The Ohio Journal, "Hazel Ridge"

Outerbridge, "Gaunt Ships"

Oyez Review, "Sophia"

Palo Alto Review, "At Faulkner's Grave"

Paper Nautilus, "Arms Fleeing Outward"

Paper Street, "Old Movies and a New Novel"

Pendragon, "Woman at a Window"

Poet and Critic, "House of Breaking Hearts"

Poetry, "As Literature Comes of Age"

Poetry South, "The Goodly Fere"

Saranac Review, "Trades"

Shenandoah, "Workshop"

Skidrow Penthouse, "Flower"

South Dakota Review, "The Descent"

Southwest Review, "Promises Not Promises"

Stoneboat, "House of Breaking Hearts"

Studia Mystica, "Poetry"

Taj Mahal Review, "Tall Buildings"

Third Wednesday, "Geometry"

Verse, "The Dime"

Contents

1

2

1

WORKSHOP

We must freshen up the language
the young poet said, so we all
came together putting our hands
one on top of another as
if we were choosing sides for
a softball game and shook and shook
the walnut tree until nuts fell
on our heads like grocery limes.

And then he said, When reading poems
aloud don't make introductions
such chunks of candy that they sour
the orange, and Dot Chevrolet said
that if a poem was not sweeter
than a chunk of candy or as
sleek as a Jaguar next to
a snow plow why risk breath at all.

Some of us went to the parking
lot, guilty with our tongues held,
and chased words up trees like dogs,
all in trouble we knew and Dot
cut a square off Sam's plug
of Brown's Mule but finding
she couldn't spit, threw her cud like
a simile against the muse.

Finding a metaphor was hard
because all the exceptions were

Ruths or Michelangelos,
but who taught trees to give nuts
Dot wanted to know while parents
of the drunk on the corner
gave him a house against the sky
and that other wall, Harvard.

THE MINOR ONES

The minor ones whose work
has come to nothing labor on,
getting seasons along below
a Montana sky, eating plantains
in a Miami furnished room.

Soiled shirts, filmed hair,
they seldom stand at microphones
or sit at tables in college
dining rooms and are never
propped for flight in airport bars.

If, as the others, they doubt
what they do, light cigarettes,
look out windows, they are not left
in rooms to wait, but wait in rooms
where no one seeks an interview.

The unsolicited heart knows
its din, the sere or mildewed
afternoons, yet on hopeless
mornings once again falters
and starts, then engines on.

WHETHER IN A COLD ROOM

Whether in a cold room
or robed by a fire
in a heavy chair,
whether with coffee
at a kitchen table

or wakeful at a corner
bar, you wrote the lines
that I read here,
listening to voices
that have survived.

Yet dead, all dead,
Wescott, Davis, Bogan,
Zukofsky, names few
I know would nod at,
grieve for, want to hear.

You wrote of what time
does not change, love, youth,
passion and decay, wrote
well to be forgotten,
so careful with your page.

I dig you up here, use
your names in a joyful way
that wakes me to your joy
and to your pain, to lines
that will not come again.

I do not know your lives
but have here today
been drawn to your breath,
the seed of the wild wheat,
the tree its shadow makes.

ARMS FLEEING OUTWARD

The tree you most want to notice
you, that's the one you study hardest,
one in close proximity in bloom.

The book whose pages stand to either
side, royal portals breathing in,
the path you weigh in scattered light.

Notice me, notice me, you may not
cry too loud, but your following
eyes keep your arms fleeing outward.

It takes many years to learn what you
would know in a second, the room
inside the window, the napkin
that you've crumpled in your hand.

FLOWER

Tight in pink-tipped bud,
the flower, nevertheless,
dances with the easy breeze
and bends and dips with the rough-
armed wind just arriving.

At home in morning dew
or in shower, it sheds
water, welcoming the wet
hands of the most ardent
rain, ducking and waving.

Most the sun, its ribbon
stealth over boxwoods, its
face intent with earnest
touch of fingers, warm,
tempting the close petals.

Daring all spring weather,
yet waiting, tight in pink-
tipped nipple, to open
only to summer when
he comes in full-dressed ease.

A NEW PLAY

Each day, even with its sameness,
is the start of a new play;
it may be the same cardinal
on the same branch in the plum, but
today the white cat wants feathers.

Or the way fog hides the same bridge
where only yesterday on way
to take his wife to her sister's,
Fred Clement's front tire blew, crashing
his new car into the railing.

Or now today, naked to the waist,
the young wife holds her husband in
her slim arms, kicking shoes away
and whispering riches that no
man could hope to coax tomorrow.

The same rain but a different
rain, dripping and slow, the same snow
and wind but today a wolf, hungry,
trotting north, following the tight
passage of wary caribou.

Actors forever the same in
the breaking dawn, stepping into
sets of altered scenery, this
day the player who sits and waits,
but tomorrow Tiresias.

CYNTHIA

As cold and distant as
before they left their tracks,
you hang there in quarter
changes. All but forgot

the night static, high pledge
rehearsed to murmur at
your surrender, frolic,
a bag of souvenirs:

as if the chase, the quest
were all that mattered, lines
bold-faced in the papers,
affair before the world.

Alone now, except for
those of us who could touch
your beauty only in
surmise, ribbons no

longer in your hair, your
focus gone, reminder of
engines fueled only
for some earthly desire.

Cold and shaken, still you
remember something else,
when all the gods of heaven
rumbled and left worse marks,

incredibly taking
this last assault in stride,
having recovered from
that day when windows were

thrown open and a boy,
too a man, was forced to
that gray capsule and made
to choose to sleep or die.

AT FAULKNER'S GRAVE

Though he'd never been there
and didn't care that those who had
sent their curious voices
to all lands saluting his name,

he raised the characters
and shook their hands and stood in overalls,
his eyes hard on the ground,
his mind fixed in the shadow of war,

not needing talk that turns
strangers friends, not needing friends
to help him understand worth
or what he liked without their praise,

living with an ancestry
not his own, adopting them, though
an outsider to all
family names and prejudices,

having his own, some of them
shed now, to exorcise as well
as he could and avoid
adornment of the wrong ones here shared,

alone as the dead one
with his brother and his guilt, though,
whatever he thought,
not his sin, knowing that those who

cleared the land could own it
only in spirit and for a short time
before the earth itself
reclaimed these fingers, this smell, this name.

OLD MOVIES AND A NEW NOVEL

Talking along this way to you
I never feel foolish, at least
not like the woman caught standing
crying to herself before her

bathroom mirror or the man in
his garage blowing on his
finger cursing the hammer he
has just thrown into the corner.

Yet there are times when what I say
makes me blush, such as "away she went
forever" or "not looking back,"
such things you know cannot be true.

What makes us say these things is not
true either, just human, the way
we want our lives to be scenes from
old movies and a new novel.

So as I talk along this way
to you, I think of the condor
riding invisible currents,
the foal being nudged to its feet

by its mother, if not human
things, the way we make them human,
as if forever happening,
as if they will always happen.

AT THE CIGARETTE STAND

Because I do not know
you, I cannot put
you down on paper;

on paper you are only
what I had to drink last
night or the sun rising.

Your hair is what we both
are, your feet one leg
balancing the other.

The words you say in
dollars are words I
say for Lucky Strikes.

Your eyes on me
are eyes for friends
or favorite brother,

eyes of your mother,
right side, rear,
in a family portrait.

I do not know you.
Here are cigarettes, not
the opening of a novel.

Please.
I do not even want
to know your name.

GEOMETRY

If you are a B, you can be
sure of never being first,
there are too many A's before you
and too many other B's.

Y's are equally cursed,
all those Z's following them;
though they can sit in shadow,
they can never be last.

B's and Y's envy most
the middle-lettered, who feel
welcome in any situation—
they are the ones telling jokes

in homeroom, those in bright colors
who drive to school, comfortable
with their C's and X's, skipping
questions that deal with location.

B's know their places, if not why
they couldn't have been quicker,
as Y's, likewise fixed and limited,
wonder why they didn't wait longer.

B is to A as Y is to Z,
who, should they notice, would
have no pity, their fortune made,
their position staid and unyielding.

THE BLANK PAGE

Now the blankness comes, waiting, like
the blankness on the trapper's hide
tilted on the wall, the blankness on
the hog's flank on the scraping board,
on the postage stamp of cheek on
the woman's face in her mirror,

waiting; waiting, blank, the husband
of fifty years trying to read
the young doctor's face, the mouth, words
of no sense, his own lips spelling
out the words, say it again, lead
him not into absurdity;

blank, the pen will not work, leaves
of fall, red and golden, 10 AD,
Winston Churchill, not an ear to
a whore, some disease, what disease!
the name, a participle can
never be a noun, speed of light;

waiting, then letters, musical
notes half-formed, partly spirited
mimeograph machine, an *e*,
faint *th*, *the*, a sentence complete,
paragraph, a round hen clucking,
stepping from her box of one egg.

Beyond the best that can be done,
beyond the pencil in the hand,
the couple kissing, the tyrant's
overthrow, the thirst for water,
earth's ether, beyond idea
and mind's metaphor, the blank page.

THE FUNNY-LOOKING MAN

There is a funny-looking man
climbing up to the capitol,
or a sequence of steps that look
as if they lead to a capitol.

He has short hair because it is
straight and would be monstrous were it
long. His nose is French like Cyrano's.
He is a funny-looking man

because he is not from our town,
or at least not *ours*; he is like
a man in the murder scene
of a movie before we know the plot.

I am a funny-looking man
and you, too, are a funny-looking
man or woman to someone,
not everyday, of course, but at least

once when you were walking up some
steps or making angel's wings
in the park, someone stopped to think,
How awful that person looks, oh god!

Perhaps it is something we need
to make us feel that we belong
somewhere, that there is one person
at least we're glad we don't look like.

He is one we know we should give
a chance, but won't, like that one from
our youth whose laugh broke our heart, who
wouldn't have touched us with a cross.

THE OLD MAN THROUGH HIS CHILDREN'S EYES REMEMBERS PAPA

The fox is rabid that
once killed our chickens that
now bites our dog. Trees aged
and fell into the road.

The path a lovely
and I once walked—where is
it? Ditches muddy still—
but where are the ditches?

Laura, Laura, this way,
I was about to show—
oh, you would have—Hell's kite,
and the dug well is gone.

It was here somewhere, Son,
the tin off the rabbit
hutch, the scar on my knee,
I swear where? where? came from.

Poison ivy, I can tell
you—open the window!
and open the window—
somebody closed the door.

TALL BUILDINGS

Of all pain perhaps the worst is
to see ourselves as fools, to hear
the whisper behind the door
or in the far corner of the room
beyond groups of otherwise faces.

If we continue with brave stances,
it is only to show we have
control in a surround of triteness,
a smile, when we were a child,
at the brown sweater at Christmas.

Home, afterwards, we, at any
cost, stay away from rooms, taking
up with objects we want no name
for, two sets of hands moving that,
to save nine, keep the head dancing.

That we are fools is no distraction.
Walking out again, we are like
a tall building, ignoring both
man and motor, preferring
more the brown river in winter.

2

TURKEY-SHOOT CHAMPION

As if notice counts, your picture
in some journal nobody
reads or everybody reads:
the marbles played for and won.

It's part of the package, pretense,
jealousy, acting what
has been played better
to few who know the difference.

If not always, take the tired man
with the long gun on his cabin
porch, turkey-shoot champion,
now a book with brown pages.

Not better to have been the loser,
not worse, a leaf one day turned,
passage dropped, seeing
in the stream of words a white stone.

The necessary blank to round it out,
for the old, the stroke, for the young,
not all blind, the happy union
of luck and youth, the urgent hope.

OPPORTUNITY

Three suns to choose from
the morning sun too cool
the noon sun too hot
the evening sun too hot still

So I chose the morning sun
to ride around in
the top laid back
until the day warmed up

I didn't know what to expect
or what I'd get
(I wasn't going to work)
but I liked having options

It didn't go of course
I parked almost immediately
rather I parked and rode
noon toward too hot still

I couldn't go back
or even to Cynthia's house
What if I belonged
to the moon after all

AS LITERATURE COMES OF AGE

Somehow, the line must be more than
it says, power cables to the house
must be umbilical cords, gyres
must be stairs winding to wisdom.

When you say the woman walked out
the door slamming it behind her,
you must be proving that women
will live in doll houses no longer.

Snakes must be phalluses, blackbirds
must be reality, swans must
be both longevity and godheads,
and Jesus himself is a dove.

Even the Three Little Pigs are
businessmen and Brer Rabbit
is a black baby outwitting
his old Southern master, Brer Fox.

England is an old bitch gone in
the teeth, and that London Bridge has
fallen down proves it, while the eagle
excretes over Latin America.

Should not mean, but be? But isn't
there in being underlying
meaning if the empty doorway
and the maple leaf mean grief?

So what we read, we must read as
something more. Maybe a thousand
years will produce ten thousand books
to help us understand each one.

For now I'll stay with youth: a boy
and girl walk in the park at dusk;
their eyes meet and their hands touch. Who
wants to know why they fall in love?

GAUNT SHIPS

The orange that in the morning sky
triggers the mind triggers mine; I
walk again in the cold hollow,
leaves down, where the bare cave beckons.

There on that morning, wind down with
no hope of rising, stripped to her
waist, Iphigenia, bound and
held by her father's soldiers, waits.

While in another town, cushioned,
shouldering a gathered gown, fed
and pampered by a dozen arms,
Helen, hair up and blond, greets Paris.

The nature of the day does not
change; we must be the character
we own, the one we have been born
and groomed to play since Pisa.

Mostly our trips to Troy are on
the gaunt ships of the Greeks as we
look out at the red dawn, sailing on,
willing to afford whatever wind.

CHOSEN TO NOTICE COLOR

The sun today has put
color into the dullest
shadows; sheds shine
like the backs of beetles

and bring us days when
porches were mopped
in spring and every heart
dreamed a red bicycle.

If, having been chosen
to notice color, we
try to ignore the sun's
indifference, we do

so knowing how much
more personal we take
its absence on cloudy
days when every limb

in the hollow is a serpent
if not dedicated
to our undoing, at least
to remind us of Adam.

But the sun goes
on shining, on all days,
and we prepare picnics,
brave the white rapids,

as that great ship, past
Neptune and Pluto now,
also ignores the darkness,
devoted to Apollo.

THE GOODLY FERE

Surely you did not think
at first, *miglior fabbro,*
to be stood in circus cage,
too hot for audience,
to be broken not as
an act but an old man.

Surely there was whimsy
in those first broadcasts, when
you had yet to learn there's
no humor in tyranny,
though authorities had proven
that in Indiana.

No one denies you were
a traitor, if being
so is to be both mad
and unpatriotic;
you committed the same
crimes against poetry.

Still, if pardoned, you will
be forgiven only
when there is an end to
tyranny, when sun no
longer spills its many
mad dances among us.

We who are slow to learn
must be broken, too, our
impatient speech silenced,
even though at first we
had thought to be as you
were once, unleashed and free.

THE EYE'S SONG

The eye in the branches
sang a song of the cheek,
peach in its marking, of
the S the body makes
stepping from clothes; and sang
of the boy on the go
glancing his comb through his
hair and the girl reading
Millay in the orchard.

The eye left the city
and the farm and sang of
suns turning on and the young
satellites jockeying.

Then the eye remembered
its place in the branches;
it blinked and, shifting
positions, sang the song
of soft changes. It sang
of red light, the black cinder.
It could not stop. The eye
of a sibyl, little
it knew it did not sing.

TODAY'S DATE

Seeing her at dusk sitting on
the porch banister smoking, he
walks up and down the street until
she notices, orders him over,
"Okay, dipshit, what do you want?"

We all know what will come of this:
they'll kiss, grow bolder, get married,
have two smartass kids, get older
and learn to hate each other.

That she'll switch from Lucky Strikes
to Virginia Slims will not change
her story, nor will the six o'clock
news, announcing future wars far
different from theirs, alter his.

And when they die, which they will in
accord with no one's protestation,
few will notice the calendar
that perhaps reads January 17, 2063.

Not quite off—they have their lives yet
before departure—they'll disregard
the things that merely matter,
their marvelous hands and speech,
her words that they'll forget, "Go home,
dickhead; there's nothing for you here."

THE COLD ONES

Here where sycophants are
not ashamed of their art,
as if others envy
or praise their gain, what room

is there for a working
desk, walls for hanging up
The Scream, or an open
door for the comic hand?

What is it all but fear
that keeps both owl and deer
to night as if peace too
is jungled in shadows?

Keeping to the wall as
in Shakespeare's day, even
if unafraid, the cold
ones go, collars up, dark

coats in the snow, taking
solace in neither drink,
work, or complaint nor in
a man or woman's love.

A HANDBOOK FOR ACTORS

Take murder, for example;
that is not interesting.
But if the victim is a young
woman partially clad
found in a lime nightgown north
of town—see, we're getting somewhere.

The waterfowl high above
disappearing into the mist
at dusk is, let's be honest, boring.
But if we take the last of
a species poached at night
by the son of a duchess for
its Chinese red feather,
we have a version that's real.

You have a mother who died?
Who cares? Reinvent her as
the lost woman who gave her life
delivering Robin Hood while
a wolf licked its paps in the forest.
A mother can be anyone,
but she is never your mother.

A story is never, face it,
its subject: it has shed its cocoon,
it is Mark Twain on stage,
Paul Bunyan with his Babe; it is
the fluttering of wings when the
magician lifts the silk from his hand.

POETRY

Not so alive and well, every
year singing less and less, cutbacks,
withdrawing patrons, the long line
of minds thumbing to Dallas or
taking the Dynasty express.

At first blaming the neighborhood:
pales edging in, reds moving out;
then the country: leaders with
rouged faces, crusades against vices,
youth with its neatly parted hair.

Then the poets: out of the open
air into rooms with vases, views
from windows, skyscapes, monks with their
private symbols, strict mortar, bricking
themselves into forgotten cells.

Why name them. Byron began the
alienation over two
hundred years ago. We could name
Shakespeare farther back, Catullus'
Lesbia, or the Greek Sappho.

It is not these things. Poetry,
black buzzard on a post, hunches
with its truth. We cannot teach it
to remember the day it folded
its dark wings, if it ever flew.

TRIAL AT AMHERST

"Today, it is my turn to speak.
Yesterday, she sat and had her
say, and said it well, but today
I take the stand. It is my day.

"Yes, I am guilty of desire.
Yes, I wear a wedding band. Yes,
I touched my hand against her hand.
Yes, I am a minister of God.

"No, I cannot say her face was
beautiful or that she had a
schoolgirl form. Was not saintly.
Had no gift for household chores.

"Maybe her eyes were brown. I saw
them blue. Maybe she liked music
and poets' portraits; I don't know
her pleasures in that other room.

"She liked flowers, if she was first
to see them bloom. And roots for tea.
Her glance away was the look that
drew me near, the coquettish words

"she wanted to seem quizzical, her
devil's way to make me blush at
God and try to take her in my arms,
her demon thoughts transferred to mine.

"I offered her life a world away
doing still the only work I
knew to do. She smiled. Of course
she would not go. She had my soul;

"what was there left for her to ruin?
I moved away. Before you judge,
play life with me. You know her words.
Pretend she has returned; she stands

"upon the walk, she calls her dog,
then, eyes on her hands, turns and asks
me to take the carriage reins. Which
of you will tell me not to go?"

LIFTING HER NAME

When I walked up the steps
to the porch at evening,
she sat in the swing singing
her own song. If I had

thought about it then, I would
have given her the same
non-glance we all did, yet
maybe would have guessed her

eyes-down need for answer.

Now, I offer that as
later option; suppose
it wasn't: a way I could
not have been, staring

into the not much longer,
the sweat to wipe away
rowing her sole voyage
and the comfort she could know

only then of freedom.

Suppose, instead, a song
devoid of reeds she sang
among, devoid of cloud,
sky, sun, the slam of door

that familiar cousins
or neighbors may have heard
but took no notice of,
the words gathering toward

concord, secret, without storm.

HAZEL RIDGE

I cross the creek
and climb the steep
path toward Hazel Ridge.
I have left him.

Not that he lied,
not that he promised
one thing he never gave,
but I cannot live
on flowers forever.

"Life is more than
a sunny afternoon,"
I told him. "And
love is more than
two hours a day."

"There are other men,"
I said, "who know that
nights make a lifetime.
From them I will marry."

I see the ridge.
Evening is coming.
I know he made
my name a song.
I know birds joined
him in singing.

And I will not forget,
but I am not wrong.
Such men are lovely
but even more lonely.
Not made for women
to live on Hazel Ridge.

PROMISES NOT PROMISES

The last click of the door
and hope is locked out,
clock stopped on the day;

promises not promises are
the longest kind of hope:
waiting, the latent knowing.

The newly blind know this,
the lame, parents after a
war department telegram.

The night to get through,
the days and days, waiting
for the past to leather.

Come with all bent things,
lingering, useless; absorbers,
slowing the door slam.

3

LIT

They rid the cave of bats,
careful, before they buy,
that there's no history
of dragon dung, no witch
that used her genitals
for joy;
        they do not clear
the lot but have it cleared,
fencing off the line of
trees where a white bull
from Crete once grazed and may
still wander secretly.

Know their mixed metaphors
quite well, brooms handy if
a spider tries a web,
wear suspenders, check for
flies and, if in season,
staff a lab;
        read papers
where a party might break
out, stomp perfunctorily
the latest thing on Joyce,
damn poets and smoke, peer
above their plastic cups.

As for Shakespeare, Dickinson
and the rest, they are but
compost for orchids in

their heads, except for James
who could feel at home in
anybody's bed;
                    power,
memos, and the buck have
added process to their work,
while that giant, once their
joy, is hushed, to sit like
Claudius by their fire.

TUESDAY

I am the day after
the fall; few birds fly that
you see, and the cat that
went for a walk is lost.

Tomorrow is a hill;
if the oak is of trees
your favorite, not one
has the art of patience.

The coffee is never
serious, getting over
a cold, one coming on,
morning of bulk rate mail.

Afternoon will be partly
sunny, evening you will
remember a lover
and dream early of Rome.

A hang around failure,
today probably, shake
out an aspirin, no
need to look at the wall.

THE DETECTIVES

Take the man in the crowd
who seems to hang off from
the rest, who watches the
door or smokes on the porch.
He's the one we're after.

Not the woman in red
dress who courts the mayor,
or lawyer with Scotch who
watches above his glass
the lady professor.

Bring him into the room
with the wooden desk, grab
his shirt and slap him twice,
as squealers were slapped in
movies in the forties.

If he won't talk, why at
first we'll offer him a
cigarette and stare out
the window ourselves or
take a walk in the dark.

When we come back, we'll piece
the things he says into
a confession, and hope
he won't think the story
good enough to get him

life, then sing out the rest.
For if he does we must
release him quick, forget
him fast and, in his case,
forgive him everything.

PUT A TITLE HERE

There is always
a setting:
the house tucked
in the cove
below the poplars,

a mowing machine
rusting in brush
higher than
the cutter bar,

and life:

the small girl
with jam
on her face
and handprints
on the front
of her dress,

wasps guarding
the holes
in their nest
and resting
upside down
with long wings.

Together they
are a play:

first the setting,
then the actors
taking turns
at being hero
and villain.

TURNER CASSITY IN ATLANTA?
I THOUGHT HE WAS IN CHICAGO

With face and hair like a woman
from the twenties on the cover
of *Vogue*, she stopped at my table:

Are you the writer or maybe
Ted Turner, she said, and I looked
from the menu into a movie.

Why, I don't know, I said, and added
quickly, Which writer? for I was
certain I was not Ted Turner.

Had she meant Turner Cassity?
I asked her. Oh, you're too old to
be him, she said. Besides, he sings.

What circle was I in? I had
never even seen Turner Cassity,
not a picture. I felt foolish.

But I do know my Dante, I
said, to make matters worse, turning
red and talking pure gibberish.

Why, he's dead, she said. You trying
to pull my leg? Well. The twenties,
cover of *Vogue*. Certainly not,

I said. Who are you then? You must
be a writer. Were we getting
somewhere? None you'd know, I confessed.

Well, you look so familiar. But
I really must go. Of course. Just
this one last thing before I do.

Do you remember Zelda? Fitzgerald's?
Why, yes. You would have made a nice
couple, she said; she waltzed, you know.

THE DIME

The man spent his life
searching for the perfect dime.

He searched in carrots
in the marketplace,
in an old woman's hands
that unwrinkled empty.

He searched in the mouths
of fishes, in a sailor's
story and on his table
in the red light of nightfall.

He searched in the toolbox
of a tractor, in the stitching
of a country girl's dress,
under a farmer's mortgage.

Always the dime was tarnished,
an apple with russet,
a frozen pond with a drowning
pool for the skating boy.

He came closest in old books:
Shakespeare had lost one,
and in paintings: Brueghel
had dropped his in the sea.

Once he was seduced by
a New England woman who said
she had a perfect dime,
but overnight it turned into
a birthmark in his pocket.

Then the current changed,
the dime began looking for
a perfect man; it was
a sign of the times.

I am calling for a perfect man,
it said. I am the voice.

But the man could not hear
the perfect dime; the dime
could not see the man.
Their cries rang through
the land hailing each other.

A GERMAN GHOST

He has come out again tonight
to tie his shoes, rest on the stone,
walk in the wet grass. Looking out
upon the lights of houses where
as a child he played, he thinks of
the sorrows that make happy days.

He walks and thinks, how love only,
facile as it now seemed, could make
morning worth the day, how the touch
of hand upon a face could make
a book, convince a people out
of work to reconstruct a state.

To spend a life, between office
and stone, upon a crazy muse
that would not be won, nor yet be
content unless she fell in every
wind to trail her drooping wing
upon the ground just out of reach.

How God is essence, the devil
in his cloak fat and unshaven,
nearly human and overrated,
how many nights in old age he
had tied his shoes in this same way
and stepped out without equal friends.

The same lone walk he must always
take, to be advisor, never
to laugh except at the waning
of his wits, this Olympian
state where in wet grass the failing
light shrivels slowly past his reach.

BEING ASKED TO SERVE AS PANELIST ON COCKLEBUR MANAGEMENT

There is no place I am not lost.
How happy it would be to be
an old explorer or oarsman
following the north star.

Awakening this morning in a house
I ought to know, I confused last
night's dream with today's comics,
understanding not one last frame.

If I sound paranoid, I am;
put me in the Alleghenies
with a compass, a possum
couldn't lead me to a sinkhole.

How would I know where seeds sprout?
No, no, no, don't ask me—
with a map and two weeks study I
might find my way to Milwaukee.

How I envy all those willing
to serve, swaying in blazers of weeds
and grasses, sure as sweetmeats
in their shucks of credentials.

LANE

Today, I know nothing that is true:
winter ends and spring comes, autumn
ends and winter returns; heroes
become old men sniveling on benches.

The water that you poured last week
from a measuring cup onto
the peace lily has dried up; the bulb
on the aging porch has burned out.

Hearing that someone is married,
someone else has died, the most inept
boy scout ever in his troupe on
the front page a lieutenant colonel.

Of course, it is summer I speak
of, spring and summer, the way
we speak of dead as passed away,
of Jesus as God, as if shards

taken from recent diggings are
Egyptian bracelets, as if
bones strung on a wire in the
Smithsonian are King of Dinosaurs.

DOROTHY'S ROOM

The morning the rooster
does not crow, nobody
dies. Death is saner
than that,
              coming any
afternoon unannounced
in open shirt, wearing
the soft loafers of a
heart attack,
              or writing
left-handed his report
standing on the black asphalt
in state patrolman's hat.

No January eve
does the dreaming girl see
the image of coming
husband's face,
              met in school
the dolt who copied her
history notes, the back
on that October night
who scored,
              or the aging
artist at the Laundromat
who does his joyless sketch
on her Beethoven shirt.

Yet we cross our fingers
on wooden heads and wear
saints' medals as we leap
the cracks,
            believing in
nothing except hope that
someday we will not grow
old enough to depend
on facts,
            live only lives
of fancied doom , then pinch
ourselves and awaken
back in Dorothy's room.

SANDWICH

The last bite he took was just
an ordinary bite from
a sandwich he'd made from something
in the refrigerator.

From something in the refrigerator
just above the celery
and below the milk and juices
he'd found what he wanted.

Laying it out on the counter,
he'd licked the knife afterwards
and placed it quietly in the sink,
running a little water.

For the rest of the house nothing
was about to happen,
the bite, after all, from an ordinary
sandwich, with some pickle.

He laid it out well and put
the knife down carefully,
not thinking whether or not he'd
run hot or cold water.

The door was closed, the bulb
out when he dropped his hand
from his mouth and danced a quiet
waltz with his shadow on the floor.

WHY I'M NOT AN ACTOR

You must let everything out, you know,
and call it genes or not, most of us
never learn to leave our socks and shirt
behind, as if no guardian
can protect what we must have back.

My friend Stan doesn't know how to tell
the truth, yet everything he says
is true the way he tells it, like after
grabbing an owl you're surprised
how thin it is without its feathers.

It's a continuation of once
slipping on the ice not being
a pro when you get up, the need
for a tree to stand behind, not letting
the fall, ache, and shock be that tree.

I'd like to be an actor like Stan,
to let myself out, then when the lights
went up, walk across the boards a real
person, the smell from my discarded shirt,
the owl after fluffing its feathers.

EXTERIORS

Finally the town was still.
It had shaken through
the seasons its lights,
its laws, its unintelligible
back street clashings, its ore,

to lie like a gashed
and burned lid among
the folds of mountains where
no coyote called at evening
and no whistle blew.

No riders leaving for
ranches with Christmas toys,
the stiff skirts of strong
women left crumpled for
their men before the fire.

No clergymen, no glass
coaches, the locked eyes of
children upon logs of feed
rattling the trap doors,
stairs at the back of stores.

Offering its peace, full
moon and quiet shadows,
lost and unimagined
in imagining, no
ghost to avenge its wrong.

JANET

The way she smoked the cigarettes
and chewed her gum, legs crossed, leaning
back on the concrete ledge beside
the tenant building steps kept us
amazed at the cliché Janet left.

We didn't know what girls thought, popping
their gum too, in packs, shooting looks
but avoiding Janet's face, not
stopping to talk to us; boys
were the only friends that Janet had.

Of course, she went bad, if bad means
doing the usual dope and drinks
and sleeping with the men with whom
you were not supposed to sleep, though
none of us had a badge to wear.

And she died, one death as good as
the rest, and always a gruesome
way to remind us of the down-
the-street, sly Mr. Rat and that
the living have much to lose.

Janet, so much alive there on
those steps, how dare we separate
the real from the romance? On stage
we all are fools—if quite unlike
your act, so bad and beautiful.

OF WHICH WE KNOW

Someone on a road walking,
never sitting or stopping
to consider the way
water flows evenly

and clearly over the flat
rocks of the narrow creek
or the way woods and field
blend with day's behavior.

Sun or moon, cloudy night
or lightning, always walking
toward or away from
beginnings or endings

of which we know only
what imagination
when active or idle
enough to surmise allows.

Their careless livelihood
equally puzzling,
always moving, never,
at least openly, naked.

Real, yet to us are they
not in their carriage at
least unintentionally
demonic, arousing

in us envy of their
misdirection and their
haughty indifference?
Or, contemplative, are

we grateful for their
remoteness, free from their
averse contamination,
as they are free from ours?

4

THE WRITER'S NOTES

"It is not what you want to write
about; it is what the voice wants
from you." Why do writers want to
write about writing when what they
ought to be writing about is
the way the sun at dawn on stones
in a desert makes the desert
look like the back of a brindled dog.

Dead centered. Too much of writing
and wanting and voice that if not
human is the way the dog sits
up and scratches its ear or bites
the tick from its side reclaiming
its own blood, if that really is
voice or just the way a carpenter,
say, drops his hammer on a nail.

The noise of words on the page should
be silent; let them be: that evening
sun goes down, the crickets give song
to the darkness, pines rising above
oaks and hickories breathe the night
air, and somewhere down a twisting
road on a dusty blanket by a stream
lovers smear their bodies on the wind.

SOPHIA

Maybe if we look at her long
enough, we can know her case, if
we give her and ourselves time, for
we're in her life now as she's in ours.

It didn't take long to get involved
though she'll never see us, never
be affected in any way by our
interest, if not our concern.

Not exactly not our concern:
though we'll never give her money
or take her hand, we see in her
a window, reflecting what's there.

One thing we cannot miss is the way
she stays to herself, perfectly
happy now that whatever was
is over, pulling on soft gloves

in winter and in summer not
afraid to show her hands again,
even if she has no garden
and no longer prefers the light.

What we learn from her we remember
a long time, some things for the rest
of our lives or, rather, as long as they
can matter or we think they do.

It is an honest distance for
seeing, not hearing her wording,
the way she's caught turning, fingers
lightly holding the back of a chair.

SHELTER

The story was not about
a dog, but a dog was its hero:
how on the one hand it was
a bitch and mated with every
breed on the block,
           and on the other
a Bruno that dug its way
out from under whatever fence.

And so you read, Well, why does
Lady stay when she knows what he'll do?
Or, You tell me what I'll feel
when the others speak of their Rex
at the kennel;
           can I take the streets'
emptiness, a house over my head
and biscuit tins in the pantry?

The hero could have been a horse,
a frost, a train, still water,
but not have been women naked
as water or men furious
as axes;
           it was a story
not of midnight or noon, an all
day story, oblique with its wounds.

BRIGHTEST, REDDEST APPLES

What bothers him most, at least
today, is the quick way things change:
yesterday his gang was the brightest,
reddest apples on the tree, faces

in tight shot needing but a splash
of water, his hands so smoothly
masculine they seemed just
modeled from a chapel ceiling;

now, it's laughs behind his back as
he comes home by way of drugstore
from the doctor's office to study
a box he's taken from his pocket.

What bothers him today is that
yesterday when recess ended,
he knew a bell would ring classes
tomorrow, learning nothing from

the death of relatives, as the sun
learns nothing from its faded neighbors,
unable to believe in his
radiance absent from the earth.

TRADES

So if I miss the poetry
in you, lay it to arrogance,
if arrogance is being too
long alone days and months on end,

forgetting intercourse with forks
that are only meals and the sun
through the open curtains that fades
the oak floor or the kitchen tile,

forgetting that the poet is
only a banker with his vault
of money, making appraisals
and stacking his parchment of loans.

So if I miss your quiet stare
to a haunted tree in summer,
lay it to one who is too much
a carpenter, his mind detached

with plans, sighting out foundation
lines, the roof's pitch, the way
design fits contour of the land,
the flying nail and hammered thumb.

The holder of mortgages does
not own the land or the builder
the homes; nor do makers of poems
own silence in an empty room.

THE WING

A dark hand was at the door.
It was not death. And when
he opened it, a mottled wing
flew toward a distant light.

Not moth, nor nightmare bat,
(nor yet a horse), it rose,
a wild let loose, a wing within
a beam upon the sky.

Arrived to say, he might
suppose, for he saw a wing
and not words, something of one in
shadowed woods, on winter

shore alone, or standing
by a tree at timber line—
romance for which the wolfer world
was slow to lift its eyes.

And for it, perhaps right.
Light fell into the dark
before his door and wing was gone,
to wait in line, in turn,

that other ring to be
dropped when he, unready,
sat on bed's edge or struck the light,
no gentler than before.

WOMAN AT A WINDOW

The rain began again.
Standing at the window,
looking out, the back of
her hand on the curtain,

she thought of last night's dream,
which came and came and came,
of her high school class, faces
young, determined and strict.

Standing there where no one
told her to stand, or not
to stand, she remembered
again the boy in the back

seat on a double date,
a boy she hardly knew,
who held her hand and kissed
her with uncertain mouth.

She had not closed her eyes
and could see, beyond the glass,
trees valleying the clear
light of her first real moon.

She tried to find his name
and what he said and where
he went, whom he married;
finally, she gave up.

Where no one told her to
stand, she watched the new rain,
faces that came and came,
thought of a line from a poem.

Was the poet who wrote it
MacNeice, some name like that,
or maybe MacLeish, who
spoke of a subway train

with a man looking out,
seeing, inching the wall,
a lone caterpillar,
butterfly waiting for wings.

FALL SEMESTER

In the coed dorms mothers
are tucking in the beds
of their freshmen sons one
last time. Fathers in their
cotton shirts have lugged their
daughters' refrigerators

and trunks to the top floors
and are resting out of
breath on lockers and crates,
or else stand in the halls
looking at bulletin boards.

The traffic cop in the street
outside continues to
give directions on the
parking of vehicles,
and the tall trees adopt
a distant green and quiet
rustle that the din of
unloading seems to deepen.

But it is mothers who are
in control here, a little
weary perhaps, out of
breath never, giving last
minute instructions on
colds, washing, parties
and a time for studying.

Finally comes the time
when time is wasted
and tomorrow is put off
until afterward (the
thousand things that are left
unsaid), while in the street
outside even the traffic
cop is kind and, for today,
filled with patience.

CAR

Today we are trading
the car. Though we have had
it a long time, we are
astonished, not just by
the price but at the taste

of want like metal in
our mouths, as if we had
everydayed our lives into
seasons where we never
thought to wish or expect.

When finally we have
agreed upon a price,
we sign some papers and take
others from the dash we know
we will not need again.

Looking at each other
and away through a world
of glass we feel the first
guilt, seeing how little we
are different from the rest,

the way we watch others
to see if they notice us,
the rush we seek from their
want, that keep-up urge we
thought that we had lost.

We wonder, speeding past,
if ever again we can
rescue our old response:
showing off, but missing
the old junker like hell.

HOUSE OF BREAKING HEARTS

This is the house about
children breaking hearts,
not your child, not your heart,
the house about children.

This is the son on the
corner, smoking, not your son,
the boy with coke in his
pockets, holding to bars.

This is the daughter who
eloped to Spain with the
writer, not your daughter,
no writer in your town.

Remember, this is not
your house; this is a house
about children, about
children breaking hearts.

This is the divorce of
parents breaking hearts,
not your parent, not your
heart, the divorce and house

about parents and children
breaking hearts. This is not
about pain in your house
nor about your divorce.

This is the fear about
children breaking hearts,
not your heart, not your child,
fear in breaking hearts;

not about your pain or
fear, not your child or house;
about pain and fear in
the house of breaking hearts.

IN THE OTHER ROOM

In the other room the table
has crystal and grapes,
meat so thinly sliced
it curls upon the plates.

In the other room there
is wine from rich vineyards
where men in loosened ties
walk up and down the orchards.

And dancing and open laughter
and quick talk of polo,
croquet over summer grass,
costumes of bright colors.

Windows with a view
and shy eyes of ladies,
hands fragile in lace
pinning on men's flowers.

Swear you would not sell
graying hair or body?
In our room sample here
the days of words and water.

COME TO NOTHING

Instead of getting high he was
drunk, sitting naked against
the alley bricks, one leg under
the other, eyes open as if dead,

the cat balanced on a dumpster
searching out the comics fish,
astonished at so white a thing,
neither soothing nor threatening.

This is what comes from expecting
something for tipping a bottle,
for pushing a bill worked
hard for across a counter,

foolish aspirant stepping from
a carriage so many gone before
have ridden effortlessly, rising
over mornings and steeple tops,

when all the while there is never
a gift a drink can buy, just
the patience of emergence, as a desert
after rain saying, Look, here I am.

THE GREAT PLATEAU

1

He reached the point
and the great plateau.
Something spoke to
him in a gray voice.

When the cold rain
began, he turned his
collar above his ears.

There was no path
through the level woods.
There was no light,
only the low voice
in the winter trees.

I know what I am
leaving, he thought.
I know the warm fires.

When night came he
sat inside a hollow
tree. There were no
bird sounds in the
forest. No mouths
against the sky,

only the gray voice
speaking low and clear.

The next day he
remembered everyone
he had ever known,
everything he had
ever seen. He
remembered a boy and
a dog. He remembered
a plow and open ring.

Suddenly his mouth
dropped. No, he
said. He zigzagged
between the trees of
the great plateau.
He tore off his coat.

It was too late.
The voice had its
teeth at his throat.

2

A half mile below
the point, a barn.
A woman is feeding
her stock. Children
are throwing hay
down from the mow.
Sometimes they stop

to stare at a gray
voice they cannot
rock from the rafters.
No matter the dark
stones they throw,
it is always there.
Sitting. Waiting.

THE DESCENT

Down the long point, on each side
the dark trees smoky under the heavy
fog, a late-summer morning.

Who can say when the descent begins,
when the blood takes a downward course,
done with flooding, as if it has pounded
and risen and fallen for this ending.

No one in the climbing, in the joy of
gaining, can be told the level ridge
that narrows in furthering; any return
fenced, gated, and locked behind.

Or the way down the long point, cutting
the dark sapling to keep from slipping,
almost happy that the heart, at last,
is spared from climbing (almost happy),
as truth quickens, blood loses its song.

PERSONAL

When I open a door
I turn the knob gently,
fling it with my hand
or pull it wide, then look
inside before I enter.

The surprises waiting to
leap out red-eyed I learned
early from my father
when air was full of autumn
and oil field meter houses.

Caution dies hard, so if
you say to me, "Let's ride
over to White Pine and go
swimming" or "Send us
a batch by late October,"

know that my suspicion
at your offered hand
is my way to reckon
with those who say, "Oh, it
will be worth your trouble."

When I open a door
I do so with foreboding,
having seen the crouched feet
on door jambs, the fisted
head cocked above the floor.

FIFTEEN

Though it doesn't divide
into a hundred evenly,
fifteen in years seems
the perfect distance:

we wake up one weekday
morning and there it is,
a face or body that
continues last night's dream,

someone asking, What are
you thinking of, Walter?
or, Grace, you seem to be
in another world today.

The shell cracks for us to
catch up with things, the gaps
in the caulk around the sink,
the shirt or dress in the closet

we will not wear again
returning again in portrait,
sugar in the salt, gold
thread in the dun sleeves.

Then looking at our hands,
or neck in the mirror, we
might still remember a pretty
name someone called us

once, even in refusal.